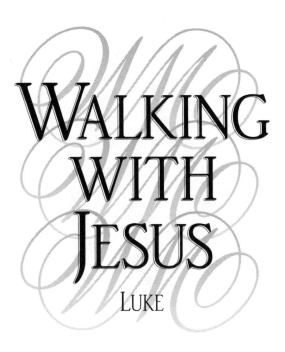

WALKING WITH JESUS

LUKE

Other Studies in the *Women in the Word* Series

Equipped for Life: Ephesians, Philippians, Colossians
Saying Yes to God: Esther
Seeing Jesus: 1–2 Peter, 1–3 John

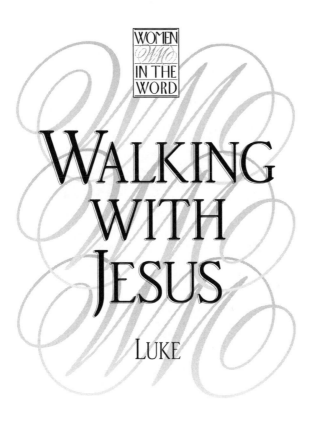

WOMEN IN THE WORD

WALKING WITH JESUS

LUKE

Linda McGinn

Baker Books

A Division of Baker Book House Co
Grand Rapids, Michigan 49516

Published by Baker Books
a division of Baker Book House Company
P.O. Box 6287, Grand Rapids, MI 49516-6287

Printed in the United States of America

ISBN 0-8010-5009-X

CONTENTS

SETTING THE STAGE FOR LUKE

The Book of Luke, driven by the actions and drama of the lives of Jesus Christ and his followers, is termed a *gospel*. *Gospel* means "good news." Darrell Bock, in the InterVarsity Commentary Series, writes, "In the gospels, theology is revealed in the context of life clothed in flesh and blood." Implementing dialogue, characterization, speeches, plot, and narrative to capture the imagination, Luke guides readers into a deeper understanding of Jesus Christ, his person, mission, and message. Luke clearly desired that his letter be a message for the Gentile. In Luke 2:14 we read, "Glory to God in the highest, and on earth peace *to men on whom his favor rests*" (emphasis added). Luke 2:32 describes Jesus as "a light for revelation to the *Gentiles* and for glory to your people Israel" (emphasis added).

Luke's goal throughout his book was to demonstrate that God's plan for salvation described in the Old Testament is fulfilled in the person of Jesus Christ for both Jew and Gentile alike. "*And all mankind* will see God's salvation" (Luke 3:6, emphasis added) highlights again that Jesus' message is to all men.

Luke was a physician, attentive to detail and accuracy in communicating God's truth. Luke was not an eyewitness of all that concerned Jesus Christ, as he indicates in the first chapter. His Gospel is "an account of the things that have been fulfilled among us, just as they were handed down to us by those who from the first were eyewitnesses and servants of the word." But because he was Paul's devoted companion, he learned of Jesus through him and those who knew Jesus intimately.

In the Book of Acts, we learn of Luke's companionship with Paul. We read in Acts 16:10, "After Paul had seen the vision, we got ready at once to leave for Macedonia, concluding that God had called us to preach the gospel to them." Other passages also make reference to Paul's relationship with Luke, including Acts 20:5; 21:1; Colossians 4:12–14; and 2 Timothy 4:11.

Luke accompanied Paul in his second missionary journey, remaining in Philippi to establish believers in the faith there (Acts 16) and then rejoined Paul in Troas following Paul's missionary journey. At that time they journeyed to Palestine together.

Luke accompanied Paul to Rome and remained with him during two years of his imprisonment. This is described in Acts 28. His association with Paul enhanced Luke's knowledge of the life and ministry of Christ.

In writing his Gospel, Luke desired to strengthen the faith of all believers, to answer the attacks of unbelievers, and to describe the good news of the gospel of Jesus Christ. He wanted to refute ill-founded reports about Jesus that were circulating throughout the Gentile world. And he wished to show that according to Jesus' teachings the Gentile Christian had a place in God's kingdom.

In his writing, Luke presented the life and ministry of Jesus Christ with historical and chronological accuracy. He directed his Gospel to Theophilus. Because the name means "lover of God," it is unknown whether this book is addressed to a particular individual or to all those who love God. Theophilus is an artistic Roman name common among government officials, a fact which encourages speculation about the letter's addressee.

As to the time of the letter's writing, some believe Luke penned his account in A.D. 58 from the city of Caesarea while Paul was imprisoned there. Others have thought it was written from Rome before A.D. 65.

Fifty percent of Luke's Gospel is unique, containing references not found in the other Gospels. Thirty-five miracles are found within all the Gospels, and Luke's narrative contains twenty of these, seven being unique to Luke alone.

Another way in which Luke's Gospel is unique is in the amount of material devoted to Jesus' closing ministry in Judea and Perea, where sixteen of the twenty-three parables occurred. As a learned man and historian, Luke, writing to both Jew and Gentile, stressed accuracy in the truth-telling of Jesus' ministry on earth.

Luke's Gospel also distinguishes itself from the others because Luke views Jesus as a man, a real human being, by using the phrase "Son of Man" twenty-four times. This is how Jesus most often referred to himself. The Gospel of John focuses on Jesus as a perfect man as well as God. Matthew's Gospel depicts Jesus predominantly as a great king. Mark portrays Jesus as an obedient servant of the Word.

The Book of Luke is most commonly divided into three parts. Chapters 1–4 contain the birth, baptism, and temptation of Jesus. The opening up of God's way of salvation and humankind's ability to approach God through Jesus Christ comprises chapters 4–18, while chapters 19–24 describe Jesus' crucifixion and resurrection.

Let's travel the dusty roads of Israel and follow the sandaled feet of Jesus. See the face of Jesus and experience the intimacy of his presence as you study his Word.

Luke 1–2

How do you respond to God when he answers your prayers and you experience the power of his intervention? Are you prepared for God's answer? Zechariah wasn't. Discover God's power in accomplishing his sovereign plan for your life and for all eternity as you read the stories of Zechariah, Elizabeth, and Mary.

Day 1

1. **Read Luke 1:1–4.**
    The truths found in the Gospels (the Good News about Jesus Christ as recorded by Matthew, Mark, Luke, and John) were collected from those with specific qualifications.

    (a) List these qualifications.

    (b) How is this described in 1 John 1:1–4?

2. Dr. Luke had a purpose in writing his book for Theophilus (whose name means "lover of God").

11

(a) Identify this purpose in Luke 1:1–4.

(b) Explain how his book can benefit you as well in the coming months.

3.   **Read Luke 1:5–17.**
       Describe John the Baptist.

───────────────────────────────── DAY 2

4.   **Read Luke 1:18–25.**
       (a) What was Zechariah's response to the Lord's word, and what were the consequences of that response?

       (b) What was Elizabeth's response to God's blessing (verse 25)?

5.   **Read Luke 1:26–38.**

(a) Contrast Zechariah's response (verse 18) with Mary's response to the angel's words. Explain the difference.

(b) We have seen the responses of Zechariah, Elizabeth, and Mary to God's Word. How do *you* respond to God when he speaks to your heart through the Bible, his Word? Take the angel's words in Luke 1:37 to be yours in faith, and pray that you might respond as Mary did in verse 38.

6.   **Read Luke 1:39–45.**

May the words of verse 45 be said of you as well.

———————————————————————————— DAY 3

7.   **Read Luke 1:46–56.**

What do you learn of God's character from Mary's words? List below those things said of God.

8.   **Read Luke 1:57–66.**

   (a) How did Zechariah act in faith against the pressure of his peers and traditions of the culture?

   (b) How did this action bring glory to God and become the first step in John's ministry (verse 66)?

9.   **Read Luke 1:67–80.**

In this passage, what was God's calling on John's life, the purpose for which he was born? Thank God now for his purposes in your life and pray to be daily sensitive to his will for you.

10.   **Read Luke 2:1–7.**

How does the taking of the census show God working in the events of history to fulfill his plans? (Refer to Micah 5:2.)

11.   **Read Luke 2:8–20.**

(a) How was the shepherds' response to meeting an angel similar to that of Zechariah and Mary?

(b) What were the angel's first words?

(c) Is your first response to meeting with God sometimes similar?

12. (a) Read the following verses. What is God's response to this understandable emotion?

Deuteronomy 1:21

Isaiah 44:8

Jeremiah 1:8

Matthew 10:31

John 14:27

Acts 27:23–25

(b) What fears toward God might be present in your life today? Ask the Holy Spirit to reveal these to you now. Pray that God's comforting words, "Be not afraid," might enable you to replace fear with faith so that you respond as the shepherds in Luke 2:15–20.

13. (a) What was Mary's response in Luke 2:19?

(b) Can you make a list now of events in your life in which you saw God's hand?

(c) Treasure and ponder these things in your heart, thank-
ing God for his working out of his eternal purposes in
your life.

———————————————————————————— DAY 5

14.   **Read Luke 2:21–40.**

Again, as with the census in the earlier part of the chapter, describe the impact of God's providential ordering
of persons and events in the words "he was named
Jesus, the name the angel had given him *before he had
been conceived*" (verse 21, emphasis added). Does this,
coupled with Psalm 139:13–16 and Jeremiah 1:5, show
that personhood begins with God before conception?

15.   **Read Luke 2:41–52.**

Even at this early age, Jesus appeared distinctively
different.

(a) Show how this was recognized by the world around
him in verses 46–47 and by his parents in verses 48–49.
Jesus' parents did not understand (verse 50).

(b) What did Jesus mean in verse 49?

16. (a) As a Christian, in what ways do you appear distinctively different from the world?

(b) Ask God to use these ways as a witness that Jesus Christ is alive in you.

LUKE 3:1–4:30

How do you face the difficulties and temptations of life? With John the Baptist's unflinching zeal and Jesus' humble authority? Learn from the examples of John the Baptist and Jesus Christ himself how to stand amid adversity and resist the devil's temptations that confront you daily.

1. **Read Luke 3:1–6.**
   What was the thrust of John's message?

2. Define the word *repentance* and the phrase *for the forgiveness of sins.*

3. **Read Luke 3:7–14.**
   What was John's message?

4.   Give examples of ways you can produce fruit in your
        life today "in keeping with repentance." Pray that the
        Holy Spirit will show you new ways each day to pro-
        duce fruit in your life.

————————————————————————————————— Day 2

5.   **Read Luke 3:15–18.**
        What was John's message about Jesus and his mission?

6.   **Read Luke 3:7–20.**
        (a) List the persons or groups of people who heard John's
            message and the response each gave.

        (b) What is your response right now to that message?

(c) Write a verse here that has specific meaning for you and explain why.

7.   **Read Luke 3:21–22.**

In this passage we see the three Persons of the Godhead (the Trinity). Identify the role of each as our one almighty God.

8.   **Read Luke 3:23–38.**

(a) List below any names in the genealogy of Jesus that you recognize from Old Testament history, and give references if possible.

(b) What do you believe was Dr. Luke's purpose in listing the earthly genealogy of Jesus when only sentences earlier he made clear that Jesus is the divine Son of God?

(c) What does Dr. Luke mean by the words in verse 23 "He was the son, *so it was thought*, of Joseph" (emphasis added)?

9.   Have you come to realize in your personal life that Jesus Christ is more than a good man, a prophet—that truly he is God "in the flesh," the Second Person of the Trinity, the Son of God? What are the implications of this truth in your personal life? How might it affect the way you live today?

══ Day 3

10.   **Read Luke 4:1–13.**
    (a) What does verse 1 say of Jesus?

    (b) How long did the devil tempt Jesus?

(c) List the three specific temptations seen in these verses.

11. (a) How do we know the devil is very aware of God's Word?

(b) What words did Jesus use to respond each time?

(c) How is this a lesson for us when we deal with temptation?

12.   With what temptations have you struggled? Can you list Bible verses which God used to help you? Be prepared to share them with your group.

13.   **Read Luke 4:14–22.**

   (a) What was Jesus' mission for his earthly ministry as fore-
       told in Isaiah 61:1–2?

   (b) What did Jesus mean in verse 21?

14.   **Read Luke 4:23–30.**

   (a) Read Mark 1:21–28 and explain what Jesus referred to
       when he said, "Do here in your hometown what we
       have heard that you did in Capernaum" (Luke 4:23).

   (b) How does Matthew 13:57–58 explain why Jesus did not
       minister in his hometown as he had elsewhere?

15.   Luke 4:26 refers to an incident in 1 Kings 17:1–15. Luke
       4:27 refers to another incident in 2 Kings 5:1–4. In each
       case God ministered to a non-Jewish person. Why does
       this explain the response of his hearers in Luke 4:28–29?

16.   How is Jesus finding faith at work in your life? Pray
        now that your faith might increase this week as you
        walk with Jesus Christ. (See Luke 17:5.)

<hr>

DAY 5

17.   What do you learn about faith from the following
        verses?

        2 Corinthians 10:15

        Colossians 1:3–5

        Colossians 2:6–7

        2 Thessalonians 1:3

1 Timothy 3:8–9

18.   What can you prayerfully do to help faith increase in your life, based on the verses above? What will you do today in this regard?

LUKE 4:31–6:11

What does it mean to be a disciple of Jesus Christ? Are you prepared to accept his challenge to follow him? Learn of the ministry of Jesus as the disciples did, watching him drive out evil spirits, heal the sick, cleanse the lepers, restore the paralyzed, and answer the questions of the religious leaders. How does being Jesus' disciple affect your life?

DAY 1

1. **Read Luke 4:31–37.**
    (a) What caused the people to be astonished at Christ's teaching?

    (b) Judging from 1 Corinthians 2:4–5, how can we speak God's Word today with power?

2. (a) Who did the demon-possessed man know Christ to be (verse 34)?

(b) How did he know this? (See James 2:19.)

(c) What did the miracle show about Christ's work (verse 36)? Also read 1 Peter 3:22.

(d) Who to this day can deliver those under Satan's bondage?

3.   **Read Luke 4:38–41.**

(a) From God's perspective, sickness can be caused by several things. How can God use even sickness (John 11:4)?

(b) Is your over-arching desire that God will be glorified in everything in your life? If not, pray that God will give you this desire and help you see life from his eternal perspective.

4.   **Read Luke 4:42–44.**

(a) In verse 43, what was Jesus' mission in life?

(b) After we have experienced the life available only in Jesus Christ (John 10:10), what should be our mission (Romans 10:14–15)?

5.   **Read Luke 5:1–11.**

From the following verses, what do we learn of the labor resulting from faith and obedience to Jesus' words?

Luke 5:5

John 11:38–40

1 Corinthians 15:58

6.   (a) Describe the disciples' action when they reached shore (verse 11).

(b) When you have come to know Jesus Christ personally, how do you regard the gains of this world? (See Philip-

pians 3:7–9.) Ask God to cause you to desire his presence and person more than anything this earth offers.

7.   **Read Luke 5:12–16.**

(a) How did the statement by the leper, "if you are willing,
you can make me clean," show his faith in who Christ
is and in his power?

(b) Why did Jesus ask him in verse 14 to tell no one? (See
Mark 1:45.)

(c) How did Jesus respond to the growing crowds in Luke
4:42 and in Luke 5:16?

8.   **Read Luke 5:17–26.**
What did Jesus see in Luke 5:20? How can faith be seen,
according to James 2:18?

9. (a) How did the Pharisees and teachers respond to Jesus in
        Luke 5:21? Read James 2:5–7 to discover the real blas-
        phemers.

    (b) Read John 5:36–39. Ask God to help you study with the
        sole purpose of seeing his Son, Jesus.

―――――――――――――――――――――――――――――――――― DAY 4

10.   **Read Luke 5:27–39.**
        Levi left everything to follow Jesus. According to Mat-
        thew 16:24, why is it imperative for all of us to follow
        Jesus?

11. (a) Explain the meaning of Jesus' words in Luke 5:31–32,
        and show how Romans 3:10 adds to this meaning.

    (b) What is your understanding of Luke 5:33–34? You might
        refer to John 3:29 for further information.

12. (a) Give your understanding of Luke 5:36–39 using Gala-
        tians 5:1, 18 and Colossians 2:10; 3:1–3 as supplements.

    (b) How does this parable apply to you personally?
        Explain.

━━━━━━━━━━━━━━━━━━━━━━━━━━━━━━━━━━━━━ DAY 5

13.   **Read Luke 6:1–11.**

       What was the law the Pharisees thought Jesus was vio-
       lating (Exodus 31:15), and for whom was the Sabbath
       made (Mark 2:27)? How do you observe the Sabbath
       each week—this special day for God? Ask God to teach
       you new ways to keep his Sabbath holy—freely and
       with joy.

14.   How are the motives of the religious leaders similar to
       those described in the following verses?

       Psalm 2:2

       Psalm 37:32; 38:12

       Jeremiah 20:10

15.   Ask God to give you pure motives and a clean heart that
       seeks to know and do his will. What is one change you
       think you should make in your life after studying this
       passage this week?

LUKE 6:12–8:56

Have the truth of Jesus and the wisdom of his teaching touched you? Do you read his Word with passive acknowledgment, or active obedience? Pause to reflect on Jesus' words in these accounts of his teaching and touching, while seeking his direction for your life.

DAY 1

1.   **Read Luke 6:12–16.**

(a) What preceded Jesus' choosing of the apostles?

(b) Why is this significant as we make decisions in our lives?

2.   **Read Luke 6:17–26.**
       This is Jesus' message to his disciples. Paraphrase verses 20–26 in your own words.

3.   **Read Luke 6:27–36.**

(a) Explain why the actions described in verses 31, 35–36 show a love and mercy that testifies to God alone.

(b) How is John 15 a key to experiencing this kind of love and mercy?

─────────────────────────────────────── DAY 2

4.   **Read Luke 6:37–45.**

(a) What are Jesus' instructions concerning criticizing and sitting in judgment on others?

(b) How can Luke 6:43–45 direct you in your relationships with others?

5.   **Read Luke 6:46–49.**

(a) What is Jesus' promise to those who come to him, hear his words, and put them into practice?

(b) What happens to those who do not?

(c) Pray that God will help you put into practice one truth from his Word three times each day.

Example: "Be merciful, just as your Father is merciful" (Luke 6:36).

Show your child mercy when a quick rebuke would have been easier.

Show your husband mercy when he returns home late from work.

Show your neighbor mercy when she has offended you.

———————————————————————————————— DAY 3

6.   **Read Luke 7:1–10.**

(a) In light of Jesus' authority, what is the deep significance of the centurion's statements in verses 6–8?

(b) Why was the faith he displayed great?

7.   **Read Luke 7:11–17.**

What do we see of Jesus' love, in verse 13, for the people he created?

8.   **Read Luke 7:18–35.**

Have you ever had doubts or second thoughts? You are not alone. John the Baptist believed yet experienced momentary doubts. How do we see this in verses 18–23?

9.   (a) How does Jesus view John in verses 24–35, even after hearing of these doubts?

(b) What were the responses of:

the people and tax collectors?

the Pharisees and experts in the law?

———————————————————————————— Day 4

10.   **Read Luke 7:36–50.**

Describe the faith and love of the sinful woman. Has your realization of Jesus' incomparable love for you despite your sin ever caused you to radically express your appreciation? (Please be prepared to share with your group.)

11.   **Read Luke 8:1–15.**
       Explain the parable of the sower and write the key verse that impresses you in this passage.

12.   **Read Luke 8:16–18.**
       Paraphrase in your own words. What is Christ's warning?

13. **Read Luke 8:19–25.**

    According to the following verses, who are Jesus' nearest relatives?
    Hebrews 2:11

    1 John 2:5

14. In Luke 8:22–25, what do we learn about the disciples' faith and the power of our God in whom we can put complete trust?

15. **Read Luke 8:26–39.**

    Demons, the angels of God's enemy, Satan, are very real. They are not some mythical creation of the Jewish mind. Paul makes this clear in Ephesians 6:10–18. Identify verses in Luke 8:26–39 that show us that Satan and his angels, though real, are defeated by Christ's word and power. Can you list any other verses?

16. **Read Luke 8:40–56.**

    (a) List the verses in this passage that show Jesus' power.

    (b) Are you depending on the power of the living Lord
        Jesus in your life today? List any particular concerns,
        worries, or fears here, and ask the Lord Jesus to help
        you trust his power to care for these needs according to
        his sovereign and perfect will.

LUKE 9—10

How do you respond to Jesus' call and instruction in your life? Who do you confess him to be when others inquire about your faith? As his disciple, his "sent out one," do you rest completely in his righteousness, or do you still find yourself attempting to justify yourself on the basis of personal achievement and performance? Learn ways to experience the joy found in dependence on Jesus and his Holy Spirit.

DAY 1

1. **Read Luke 9:1–9.**

   Jesus gave the disciples several things in this passage. List these things and describe the mission on which they were sent.

2. **Read Luke 9:10–27.**

   When the disciples returned and Jesus wanted to be alone with them, crowds followed. In Luke 9:10–17, how did Jesus respond to the multitudes?

3. (a) In Luke 9:22–27, Jesus clearly declared who he was and
        the mission he was to complete. Read this prayerfully.
        Explain his person and mission.

    (b) How do Peter's words in verse 20 affect your life today?

4.   **Read Luke 9:28–36.**
        The question posed by Herod in Luke 9:9 is answered
        by Peter in verse 20 and confirmed by Jesus' transfigu-
        ration and continued miracles. How does this passage
        confirm for the disciples, and for you, that Jesus is God's
        Son? List verses that are particularly significant to you.

5.   **Read Luke 9:37–45.**
        In verse 44, why do you think Jesus spoke the words that
        he did at the moment when "they were all amazed at the
        greatness of God" and were "marveling at all Jesus did"?

6.   **Read Luke 9:46–62.**

In verse 51 we see Jesus' consuming interest. List the words of Jesus in these verses that explain what it means to follow him—the truths so important to him as he knew his time on this earth was growing short. Are you seeking to follow Jesus as he describes here?

——————————————————————————— Day 3

7.   **Read Luke 10:1–24.**

Explain the significance of the following verses.

Verse 2

Verse 6

Verses 11–12

Verses 13–14

Verse 16

Verse 20

Verse 22

Verse 24

8.   What do you find to be the source of Jesus' joy in Luke
        10:21? Do you think of Jesus as joyful? Why or why not?

9. (a) Write key phrases concerning joy and the Lord Jesus
        from the following verses.

John 15:9–11

John 17:13

Acts 14:17

Acts 16:34

Romans 14:17

(b) Ask the Lord Jesus to give you his joy through his Holy
Spirit.

━━━━━━━━━━━━━━━━━━━━━━━━━━━━━ DAY 4

10.   **Read Luke 10:25–37.**
        What do we learn about testing Jesus (verse 25) and
        desiring to justify ourselves before him (verse 29)?

11. (a) Describe ways a person might test Jesus in a wrong way.

(b) How do we justify ourselves before others, and sometimes before God, when we have been convicted about an area in our lives needing change?

12. What is Jesus' message to you personally in verses 30–37? Is there someone in your life today to whom you should reach out in a new way and show mercy?

─────────────────────────────────────── Day 5

13. **Read Luke 10:38–42.**
Do you take time each day to stop everything and listen to Jesus?

14.   Have your responsibilities gotten out of perspective? Are you driven by these rather than being led to the Lord Jesus? Ask the Lord Jesus to show you the freedom found in Matthew 11:28–30. Ask him for a new realization that even the work and responsibilities of your day can be done through his strength and with his fellowship.

LUKE 11–12

Consider your communication with God. Is prayer a constant conversation with God, or a rarely spoken request offered with fear and timidity? Learn more about prayer and intimacy with God through Jesus' teaching as you prepare for Jesus' return.

DAY 1

1.   **Read Luke 11:1–4.**

       In your own words, paraphrase each phrase of the model prayer Jesus gave his disciples.

       Father,

       hallowed be your name,

       your kingdom come.

       Give us each day our daily bread.

       Forgive us our sins,

for we also forgive everyone who sins against us.

And lead us not into temptation.

2.   **Read Luke 11:5–8.**
    (a) What do Jesus' words tell us about persistence in prayer?

    (b) List here three of your deepest heartfelt concerns. Pray boldly about these each day this week, asking God in his mercy to work his perfect will in each of these situations. .

── DAY 2

3.   **Read Luke 11:9–13.**
    What are Jesus' promises in these verses?

4.   Verses 9–10 can be misinterpreted as meaning God will
        give us *anything* we ask for (perfect health, problem-free
        relationships, etc.). But Luke 11:2–4 shows us first what
        our priorities should be in prayer.

    (a) Explain Luke 11:9–10 in light of Matthew 6:33.

    (b) What great gift, according to Luke 11:13, will our Father
        in heaven give abundantly to those who ask?

5.   **Read Luke 11:14–28.**
        There was conflict among the people regarding Jesus'
        authority. Beelzebub is another name for Satan. Read
        Matthew 12:28 along with Luke 11:20 and identify by
        what power Jesus drove out demons.

6. (a) According to Luke 11:24–26, what happens when an evil
        spirit is cast out of a person but the Holy Spirit does not
        come to dwell in him?

    (b) Pray as Jesus describes in Luke 11:23, and ask the Holy
        Spirit to fill and control your life today so that God's
        will for your day will be done (Ephesians 5:18).

7.   **Read Luke 11:29–36.**

   (a) According to verse 34, why is it important that we are
       careful about what things we allow to enter our minds
       through TV, newspapers, novels, and magazines?

   (b) What does verse 33 tell us about being shining lights of
       the gospel to those around us?

8.   **Read Luke 11:37–12:3.**

   (a) List the six woes Jesus tells the Pharisees.
       1.

       2.

       3.

       4.

5.

6.

(b) Ask God to cleanse you from those hidden things on the inside today so you can be a clean vessel of his light and truth.

─────────────────────────────────────── Day 4

9.   **Read Luke 12:4–12.**
   (a) Whom are we to fear and *not* to fear according to verses 4–7?

   (b) What are Jesus' warnings and comforts in verses 8–12?

10.   **Read Luke 12:13–21.**
   What do we learn about greed? What does it mean to be "rich toward God"?

11.   **Read Luke 12:22–34.**

   (a) List phrases of comfort.

   (b) Why is worry worthless?

(c) Ask God to show you any fear, greed, or worry that you
are harboring today. Ask him to deliver you from these
things that hinder you from placing your complete trust
in him. Take hope in Psalm 27:1 and thank God for his
freedom from these crippling emotions (fear, greed, and
worry).

—————————————————————————————————— DAY 5

12.   **Read Luke 12:35–48.**

In verse 40, what are Jesus' directives concerning his
second coming, his final return to the earth?

13.   **Read Luke 12:49–53.**

What is the difference between the peace described by
Jesus in this passage and the peace spoken of in Luke
2:14?

14.   **Read Luke 12:54–59.**

(a) Explain Jesus' words in light of those who refuse to recognize that he is the Son of God, the Messiah, God's
way of salvation.

(b) Choose one verse that had the greatest impact on you this week. Ask the Lord to enable you by his Holy Spirit to obey Jesus' words written in this verse.

LUKE 13–14

Jesus spent much time instructing those who came to him with parables. Parables were created to convey his eternal truth in tangible, easily understood illustrations familiar to everyday life. Parables are to permeate our souls just as daily experiences permeate our lives. Has one of Jesus' parables permeated your soul lately? Consider this chapter as an opportunity to experience God's truth in a way that affects the deepest elements of your daily life.

DAY 1

1. **Read Luke 13:1–9.**

   (a) Who is guilty of sin according to this passage?

   (b) Are there degrees or grades of sin, or can God's judgment better be compared to the pass/fail system? (See James 2:10.)

2.   How does verse 9 in this passage show the mercy of
        God?

3.   **Read Luke 13:10–17.**
   (a) In one sentence of ten words, summarize Jesus' mes-
       sage.

   (b) How would you define the word *hypocrite*?

   (c) Ask the Lord to reveal any judgmental attitude you have
       which causes you to look down on another Christian.
       Ask for his forgiveness and cleansing so that you may
       see this person in a new light.

=== DAY 2

4.   **Read Luke 13:18–21.**
        What do you learn about the kingdom of God?

5.   **Read Luke 13:22–30 and Matthew 7:13–14.**

(a) Who or what is the narrow door of salvation? (Read
John 10:9; Acts 2:21; Romans 10:13.)

(b) On what basis will some people try to enter the kingdom after it is too late (verse 26)?

6.   **Read Luke 13:31–35.**

(a) In Luke 13:34, what are Christ's feelings toward those
who refuse to enter through the narrow gate?

(b) What are the repercussions of rejecting God's only plan
for salvation (verse 35)?

(c) Have you entered through the narrow gate yet? If not,
do so in prayer today. If you are unsure, call your Bible
discussion leader for help. If you have already entered,
pray for a family member or friend who has not.

7.   **Read Luke 14:1–6.**

   (a) Based on your previous study of this book, why do you
       think the Sabbath is so important to Jesus?

   (b) What is Jesus' message to the religious Pharisees over
       and over again concerning this subject?

8.   **Read Luke 14:7–11.**
       What is Christ's clear directive about pride in this pas-
       sage? (Paraphrase Luke 14:11.)

9.   **Read Luke 14:12–14.**

   (a) What do we learn about hospitality?

   (b) God wants us to apply his truth. Which of the above
       passages do you believe God wants you to apply
       today (something concerning the Sabbath, pride, or
       hospitality)?

(c) Suggest three ways you can apply this one truth this
    week. Ask God to help you be a doer of his Word, and
    not just a hearer. (See James 1:23–25.)

━━━━━━━━━━━━━━━━━━━━━━━━━━━━━━━━━━━━━━ Day 4

10.   **Read Luke 14:15–24.**
       How can ties to our earthly world keep us from answer-
       ing God's invitation of salvation (see verses 18–20)?

11.   Each person has a lifetime to respond to God's invita-
       tion of salvation. What happens to those who reject that
       invitation?

12. (a) Though many will reject God's invitation, what is our
    responsibility as God's servants to extend his invitation
    (verses 21, 23)?

    (b) Is there anyone in your life today whom God wants you
    to tell about himself? Ask him, and then tell him that
    you will obediently accept that responsibility. Pray for
    his Holy Spirit's direction, wisdom, and guidance.

═══ DAY 5

13.   **Read Luke 14:25–27.**

        Jesus gives two directives for us to be his disciples. *Hate*
        is a comparative word in this passage. One must be
        more important to you than the other. What does it
        mean to carry your cross and follow Christ?

14.   **Read Luke 14:28–33.**

        The decision to follow Jesus Christ is a permanent one,
        made soberly. How does this passage explain this?

15. **Read Luke 14:34–35.**

   (a) How do these verses show that God expects the decision to follow Christ to be a permanent, lasting one?

   (b) Ask God to help you commit *all* of yourself to him, completely and permanently. He alone is life, and anything less than a total commitment leaves existence on earth both worthless and futile.

LUKE 15–17

Do you desire a glimpse at the heart of God? That is your privilege every time you open the Bible. The Holy Spirit desires to reveal God's character to you each time you open its pages. Read the parables of Jesus in this section with a specific desire to see God's face and identify his person.

── DAY 1

1. **Read Luke 15:1–32.**

   Explain in one sentence of fifteen words or less the meaning of each parable in the following verses.
   Verses 3–7

   Verses 8–10

   Verses 11–31

2.   How are these parables a response to the Pharisees' muttering in verses 1–2?

3.   (a) What do we see of the character of our heavenly Father in these parables? (See especially verses 11–31.)

     (b) Thank your Father now for his heart of love and compassion toward you. Do you see him this way each day? Pray that you will.

─────────────────────────────────────── Day 2

4.   **Read Luke 16:1–15.**
       People are more important to God than money, and our stewardship of money should be governed by God's priorities instead of our own. Choose the verses from this passage that explain this.

5.   What was the response of the Pharisees (verse 14)? Explain the meaning of verse 15.

6.   **Read Luke 16:16–18.**

The phrase "forcing his way" (verse 16) probably speaks about the fierce earnestness with which people were responding to the gospel of the kingdom. What do we learn in this passage about Christ's teaching concerning the following?

Verse 16—the era of the Law and the Prophets, a new era beginning with John

Verse 17—God's Law

Verse 18—divorce

7. (a) Why is the reality of forgiveness in Christ (introduced by John) such a needed message in our world today,

when people so blatantly break God's law and reject God's best for their lives?

(b) Ask God to give you an opportunity to extend his forgiveness to someone this week.

Day 3

8. **Read Luke 16:19–31.**

From this passage, describe the very real place called hell.

9. We have a lifetime of opportunity to place our faith in Christ. Why does Abraham know assuredly that people will even reject One who is thoroughly acquainted with heaven and hell, comes to warn them (verse 27), and actually rises from the dead (verse 31)?

10. (a) Does the reality of an actual hell spur you to be more fervent in telling loved ones and others about God's

plan of salvation through Jesus Christ alone? Why or why not?

(b) If you have never faced the reality that hell is a real place where those who reject Christ are destined to go, ask God to make this truth real to you. Pray that God will help you to be more concerned for those around you, and ask for an increased desire to witness.

=================================== DAY 4

11.   **Read Luke 17:1–19.**

(a) Why is the personal witness of our lives so important to others?

(b) Why does our forgiveness of others reflect, maybe more than anything else, God's message to the world?

12.   What do we learn about faith in Luke 17:5–6?

13. (a) How does the attitude of the thankful leper in Luke
        17:11–19 contrast with the parable in Luke 17:7–10?

    (b) How does recognition of God's mercy and a grateful
        heart relate to faith (verse 19)?

    (c) Pray today as the disciples did in Luke 17:5: "Lord,
        increase my faith."

── Day 5

14.   **Read Luke 17:20–21.**
        Explain Jesus' meaning in these verses. How does this
        apply to you?

15.   **Read Luke 17:22–37.**

Jesus speaks of three periods in this passage. Describe each according to the following verses.

(a) The present—verse 25

(b) The period before his coming—verses 22–23

(c) The day of Jesus' second coming to earth—verses 24, 26–37

16. (a) What do you learn from the following passages about Jesus' coming again?

Matthew 24:3–35

Mark 13:5–31

1 Thessalonians 4:16–5:11

2 Thessalonians 2:1–15

(b) How can you be prepared for Christ's coming? Are you prepared today?

LUKE 18–19

What are Jesus' last words as he approaches the end of his time on earth? What message seems most compelling? Consider the words and actions of Jesus as he prepares each of us to live by faith in his presence, awaiting his imminent return.

DAY 1

1. **Read Luke 18:1–8.**

   What was Jesus' purpose in telling this parable to the disciples?

2. God will always care and act justly toward you (verses 7, 9). Will you exercise your faith in response to him (verse 8)? List ways you can exercise your faith this week.

71

3.   **Read Luke 18:9–14.**

   (a) For whose benefit did Jesus speak this parable?

   (b) Describe the two men mentioned in this parable. What difference in attitude separated the men?

   (c) Ask God to give you an attitude of humble reliance on him today.

-- DAY 2

4.   **Read Luke 18:15–17.**

   What is the meaning of Jesus' phrases "for the kingdom of God belongs to such as these" and "receive the kingdom of God like a little child"?

5.   **Read Luke 18:18–30.**

   The rich ruler seemed to have everything, especially position and possessions. What was lacking in his life?

6.   Write your thoughts about verse 27. Do you believe
        Jesus' statement here in light of the impossible things
        in your life? Are *you* trusting God with the impossible
        today?

――――――――――――――――――――――――――――― Day 3

7.   **Read Luke 18:31–34.**

        In this passage, Jesus describes what the future holds
        for him. Explain how the following verses "written
        by the prophets" foretell what Jesus describes in this
        passage.

        Psalm 22:6–8, 11–18

        Isaiah 53

        Zechariah 13:7–9

8.   **Read Luke 18:35–43.**

(a) How did the blind man display persistent faith?

(b) Jesus knew what the man wanted before he said, "What do you want me to do for you?" because he knows all things. Why do you think he asked the question?

9.   Is Jesus asking you today, "What do you want me to do for you?" Are you afraid to ask because of lack of trust and faith? He can accomplish anything that is in accord with his will. Ask according to his Word today, and if you are unsure of his will, pray according to James 1:5–8.

—————————————————————————————— DAY 4

10.   **Read Luke 19:1–10.**

(a) What do we learn about Zacchaeus's hunger for God?

(b) How did Zacchaeus respond to Jesus?

11.   Explain Jesus' words in verses 9 and 10.

12.   **Read Luke 19:11–27.**
    (a) How does Jesus use this parable to show us how to use
        his gifts until he comes again and the kingdom of God
        is completely established on earth?

    (b) Are you allowing God to work in and through your life
        for his glory, or have you buried his talents and gifts
        with words like, "Oh, I can't do that . . . I don't have any
        gifts . . . I just don't have time . . . God certainly wouldn't
        want to use me"? Ask God to help you identify his gifts
        to you and to use them according to his will.

————————————————————————————————— DAY 5

13.   **Read Luke 19:28–44.**
        The closing events of Jesus' life were now beginning.
        How do verses 30–35, 40, and 42–44 show that God's
        plans would not be hindered?

14.   How does Job 42:2–6 (particularly verse 2) confirm the
       guaranteed nature of all the events soon to occur in
       Jesus' life?

15.   **Read Luke 19:45–47.**
    (a) How did the following people act as the final stage of
        God's plan was being revealed?

       "Temple robbers"

       Chief priests, teachers of the law, leaders

       People

(b) Describe the same types of people in our world today, and ask God to help you witness to them since Jesus' second coming is imminent.

LUKE 20–22

Jesus' mission is nearly accomplished. The events laid out before the beginning of time move into actuality. How does Jesus approach these stressful times? How do you approach the stressful times in your life? Observe Jesus' attitudes, words, and actions as you develop a strategy for facing stressful events in your life. Let his example determine your course.

DAY 1

1. **Read Luke 20:1–8.**

   Explain how Jesus' question exposes the hypocritical flaw in the lives of the chief priests and teachers of the law.

2. **Read Luke 20:9–19.**

   (a) What is the meaning of this parable?

(b) What will happen to those in every generation who reject Jesus Christ, God's Son?

(c) God mercifully sent his Son to a people (the human race) whose actions and attitudes rightfully deserve his judgment and the penalty of death. According to your study of Luke, is faith in Jesus Christ God's only provision for salvation? Have you accepted God's provision or are you still waiting and evaluating? There is no neutral ground. Those who do not accept Jesus Christ have, by their neglect, rejected him. Ask God to help you each day to walk in fellowship with Jesus, accepting and experiencing his perfect will for your life.

DAY 2

3.   **Read Luke 20:20–26.**

(a) The spies of the religious establishment met face-to-face with the supernatural wisdom of God. How did they respond?

(b) Read the following verses and note phrases that show God understands our every thought and motive.

Psalm 94:11

Isaiah 55:8–9

Hebrews 4:12–13

4.   Our thought life is important to God. Philippians 4:8 gives
        us a standard for judging our thoughts. Ask God to
        cleanse you of unclean or unkind thoughts today, help-
        ing you to monitor those thoughts that go into your mind
        (through TV, magazines, and movies) and to fill your
        mind with thoughts like those found in Philippians.

5.   **Read Luke 20:27–47.**
        In the following verses, how do the religious leaders
        attempt to elevate themselves while putting down Jesus
        (which they never succeeded in doing)?
        Verses 27–39

        Verses 40–44

        Verses 45–47

6.   **Read Luke 21.**
        In one sentence of ten words, summarize Jesus' message
        concerning his second coming.

7.   List here the signs Jesus describes that show when his
        coming is imminent.

8.   (a) What are Jesus' instructions in verses 34–36 for our daily
        behavior?

(b) What thought strikes you personally concerning these verses?

9.　**Read Luke 22:1–6.**

Who more than Judas or the chief priests and teachers wanted to kill Jesus (verse 3)? Why?

10.　**Read Luke 22:7–38.**

(a) In verses 7–13, how do we again see God's plans unfold?

(b) According to verses 14–22, what is the significance of the communion that you take in church?

11. (a) In verses 31–32, what comfort is found for you and me when we realize that we, too, will fail in fulfilling God's perfect plans for us?

(b) Jesus gives the disciples new orders in Luke 22:35–38 (see the old orders in Luke 9:3–5 and 10:2–16). Matthew 10:5–42 expands on Luke's account of these new orders given to the disciples. How do Jesus' words in Luke 22:35–38 show that the time has come when the events in Matthew 10:16–23 will soon be fulfilled?

(c) Is there a situation in your life where Matthew 10:16 would be a word of wisdom to you today?

━━━━━━━━━━━━━━━━━━━━━━━━━━━━━━━━━━━━━ Day 5

12.   **Read Luke 22:39–53.**

(a) List chronologically the events recounted in these verses.

(b) Why do you think Jesus so intensely wanted the disciples to pray?

13.   **Read Luke 22:54–62.**

Imagine that you are Peter. Write a paragraph describing your experience. Include the emotions and feelings you believe he would express.

14.   **Read Luke 22:63–71.**

(a) Jesus embodied *truth*. How did the following people respond to truth?

Men who were guards

Whole council of elders

(b) Jesus Christ and his Word are absolute truth. The world may deny it, reject it, and distort its appearance, but it cannot change it. Are you afraid of God's truth examining your life? Don't be! God is not only truth and holy justice but loving mercy. Ask for his mercy and a deeper desire to live by his truth unashamed. Read John 3:17–21 for assurance (especially verses 18 and 21).

LUKE 23–24

Living out one's faith in difficult times begins this week's discussion as we consider the life of Joseph in Luke 23:50–56. We then evaluate our responses to God as he lives and works in and through our lives. Do we believe God and his promises, anticipating his answers to our prayers? Finally, do we recognize the living Lord Jesus Christ's active involvement in each moment of our lives, and do we thank and praise him for his presence? How can we show our love for Jesus more effectively?

=== DAY 1

1.   **Read Luke 23:1–25.**

       What do you learn of Pilate and Herod in this passage?
       (Remember Herod was the one who rejected the convicting message of John the Baptist and beheaded him.)

2.   **Read Luke 23:26–43.**
        Which of the criminals understood the significance of
        verse 38 and responded accordingly?

3.   **Read Luke 23:44–49.**
    (a) How did each of the following respond to Jesus' death?
        Creation (verse 44)

        God the Father (verse 45)

        Jesus (verse 46)

        Centurion (verse 47)

        All the people (verse 48)

Women believers (verse 49)

(b) What significance does Christ's crucifixion hold for you today? Thank Jesus Christ again for paying this price so that you may spend life with God forever.

4.   **Read Luke 23:50–56.**
        Joseph was a believing man amid the religious leaders. How did he live out his faith in obedience to God?

5.   (a) How do we see the believing women's faith lived out in these verses?

     (b) How did their keeping of the Sabbath amid tragedy and grief show their faith and obedience to Jesus' teaching?

6.   Ask God now to show you ways that you can live out
        the faith within you before your peers and the world
        around you. List your thoughts.

═══════════════════════════════════════ DAY 3

7.   **Read Luke 24:1–12.**
        (a) When Jesus did exactly what he had promised, how did
             these people respond?
        The women

        The Eleven

        Peter

(b) Do you ever have a similar response when God accomplishes his work in your life, answering prayer according to his promises?

8.   **Read Luke 24:13–35.**

Jesus Christ is alive today in the same way he was when he appeared to these men. He rose from the dead once for all, and he remains just as alive today as he was then. Are *we* foolish and slow of heart to believe (verse 25)? May our eyes, like the eyes of the men in this passage, be opened to recognize him (verse 31). Pray that your eyes will be open to see Jesus in a deeper way as a result of your study.

── DAY 4

9.   **Read Luke 24:36–44.**

What did Jesus do to remove doubt, provide undeniable proof of his resurrection, and confirm the truth of every word said during his daily ministry with his disciples on earth?

10.   **Read Luke 24:45.**

(a) Who alone makes us able to understand the Bible?

(b) Ask the Lord to open your mind more each day to understand the Scriptures.

━━━━━━━━━━━━━━━━━━━━━━━━━━━━━━━━━━━━━━ Day 5

11. **Read Luke 24:45–53.**

    Does the fact that Jesus Christ is *very* alive and involved in your daily life (praying for you, loving you, caring for you) bring you great joy? Are you praising God today for the love that the Lord of the universe has for you? If not, ask God to warm your heart to his love and care for you.

12. What can you do in response to that love? Read the following verses, writing down phrases that give you direction.

    Luke 24:46–49

    Matthew 28:18–20

    Mark 16:14–20

    John 21:15–19

For more information, supplementary resource materials, and audio tapes concerning the formation and maintenance of vibrant, effective, small and large group Bible studies, please contact:

Roz Soltau
Women in the Word
   Ministries
(954) 782-7506

Karen Vander Elzen
Living in the Word International
P.O. Box 8998
Asheville, NC 28814
1-800-948-0745 or
(704) 645-5115